STOP, LOOK, AND WRITE!

EFFECTIVE WRITING THROUGH PICTURES

BY HART DAY LEAVITT
AND DAVID A. SOHN

BANTAM BOOKS

BANTAM PATHFINDER EDITIONS

NEW YORK / TORONTO / LONDON

07943

ENGLISH LANGUAGE -- RHETORIC.

RLI: VLM 6.0
IL 7.12

STOP, LOOK, AND WRITE!
Bantam Pathfinder Edition published November 1964

Library of Congress Catalog Card Number: 64-7920

LEARNING TO WRITE = LEARNING TO SEE!

Here is a unique new method of learning to write that is as revolutionary as it is simple. Based on the principle that all effective writing depends primarily on accurate, insightful observation, it teaches the student how to see life with the perceptive eye of the great photographer. Then, the student learns how to express himself and what he has observed in an entirely fresh and original way. Included are examples of the work of such famous photographers as Robert Capa, Edward Steichen, Henri Cartier-Bresson, Philippe Halsman, Marc Riboud, and many Scholastic Magazine Photography Award prize winners.

STOP, LOOK, AND WRITE!
THE CREATIVE WAY TO LEARN WRITING

BANTAM PATHFINDER EDITIONS

Bantam Pathfinder Editions provide the best in
fiction and nonfiction in a wide variety of
subject areas. They include novels by classic
and contemporary writers; vivid, accurate
histories and biographies; authoritative works
in the sciences; collections of short
stories, plays and poetry.

Bantam Pathfinder Editions are carefully
selected and approved. They are durably bound,
printed on specially selected high-quality paper,
and presented in a new and handsome format.

THE AUTHORS:

HART DAY LEAVITT is a graduate of Yale University. Since 1937 he has
taught English at Phillips Academy, Andover. He is also editor of two books
for the Looking Glass Library.

DAVID A. SOHN is Instructor of English in Middlesex High School, Darien,
Connecticut, and Assistant Supervisor of Study Skills, The Study Skills
Office, Yale University. He is also the editor of TEN TOP STORIES, REVO-
LUTION IN TEACHING, and PROGRAMS, TEACHERS, AND MACHINES.

Contents

Introduction 7

SECTION ONE: The Image of Concentration . . . 11

SECTION TWO: First Try 15

SECTION THREE: The Power of Observation . . . 21

SECTION FOUR: The Art of Inventing Titles . . . 29

SECTION FIVE: The Art of Comparison 35

SECTION SIX: Contrast 47

SECTION SEVEN: Word-Pictures 59

SECTION EIGHT: Emphasis 69

SECTION NINE: Point of View 79

SECTION TEN: Seeing an Idea 89

SECTION ELEVEN: Conflict 97

SECTION TWELVE: Character 107

SECTION THIRTEEN: Dialogue 121

SECTION FOURTEEN: A Good Story 129

SECTION FIFTEEN: The Unexpected 141

SECTION SIXTEEN: Moving Word-Pictures . . . 149

SECTION SEVENTEEN: The Other Senses 161

SECTION EIGHTEEN: Imagination 169

SECTION NINETEEN: Corn 179

SECTION TWENTY: Humor 189

One Final Exercise 197

The Students Write 203

Coda 221

"What a strange way to learn to write: studying photographs!" It will surely seem strange if you never thought of the connection between language and seeing. Actually, the way you select words and organize them into whole compositions depends on the way you see human experience. If you literally do not see anything, you will of course have nothing to say.

The student who writes the following kind of prose —because he doesn't "see" anything better to write about —will always have a difficult time expressing himself, and he will be dull and bored:

> The main reason I like stamp collecting is that it is very interesting. I can always sit down and look over my collection; or if the latest stamp magazine is around I can look at that and read about the quotations of prices. If I find a stamp in the auction I want, I will look it up in a catalogue, find the price of it, and think what I should bid.

Such a student, if he never learns how to be more observant, very easily grows up into the sort of adult who on the witness stand, drives lawyers into straitjackets:

> "Mr. Acorn, will you tell the jury just what the man looked like?"
>
> "Well, it's hard to say . . . he was kind of . . . dark, I guess . . . had on a medium-colored suit . . . sort of . . . he wasn't really tall, but he wasn't short either . . . and he had on one of those what-you-call-it hats . . . had a funny way of speaking, too . . . sort of like . . . like . . . kind of . . . well. . . . You know what I mean. . . ."

On the other hand, anyone who has learned to observe, like the author of the following paragraph, is neither dull nor bored; for she has learned a superior way of seeing and writing:

Annabel and Midge came out of the tea room with the arrogant slow gait of the leisured, for their Saturday afternoon stretched ahead of them. They had lunched, as was their wont, on sugar, starches, oils and butter-fats. Usually they ate sandwiches of spongy new white bread greased with butter and mayonnaise; they ate thick wedges of cake lying wet beneath ice cream and whipped cream and melted chocolate gritty with nuts. As alternates, they ate patties, sweating beads of inferior oil, containing bits of bland meat bogged in pale stiffening sauce; they ate pastries, limber under rigid icing, filled with an indeterminate yellow sweet stuff, not still solid, not yet liquid, like salve that has been left in the sun.

—DOROTHY PARKER, "The Standard of Living"

What this book proposes to do is provide a method whereby both students and adults can learn something about the art and power of observation. You might call the method "A Beginners' Course in How to See." To "notice," to "perceive," to "see" in the best possible way, one needs to practice looking for such things as similarities, differences, emotions, gestures, colors, details, and conflicts. They are all part of the technique of the art of observation. Archibald MacLeish, the poet, has cited the goal: it is to learn to "see feelingly."

Every picture in this book has been chosen not only as a test of the ability to see merely literal things, but of the art and power to see the intangibles: character, feeling, images, ideas, innuendoes, and other ESP's. Difficult as they are to find, and to discuss, they could not be ignored in a book like this—a book on the power of observation—since they are really the main reason why anything is superior, good, and great, whether it is a movie, a book, a photograph, a bit of conversation, or a student "theme."

To speak strictly in educational terms for a moment, there has been much too much emphasis, both in teaching

d in textbooks, on the learning of rules, especially
ayune and mechanical ones—like the use of "like"—
d not nearly enough stress on the kind of subject mat-
to which a student should apply the rules. Rules are
t enough; a new approach is needed to help boys and
ls find something lively and meaningful to write about.
rough the study of photographs, this book aims to
courage young people to use their senses to discover
ngs worth writing about, in precisely the same way
at a good professional writer does.

To be very specific, one of the first lessons a profes-
nal newspaperman or a free-lance photographer learns
the importance of "human interest," or what is known
ong journalists as a "nose for news." What this book
oposes is that students discover "human interest" by
dying pictures taken by trained observers who know it
en they see it.

Finally, this book is also about language. This is the
ucial test: NOT just—Have you seen accurately and
aginatively?—BUT: Have you used language that
ithfully and fully communicates to someone else?

Everything here aims at the expression of meaning in
e most effective possible way, and this "meaning," this
sult of observation, must always include the PARTICU-
AR, the SPECIFIC, the DETAIL. One of the main rea-
ns for using photographs here is that they emphasize
articular details with staggering force, so that eventually
yone addicted to old abstractions like "good," "neat,"
wonderful," "nice," and "queer" will see how futile they
e, both as descriptions of the sharp reality in the pic-
res, and of the same sharp reality in human experience.

The original idea for this book was developed through
early ten years of experiment with high-school students.
the process of preparing the presentation, it gradually
ecame quite clear that the essential philosophy is ap-
licable to anyone, whether in school or out, young or old,
mateur or professional. Each one can learn the power
f expression from the art of observation.

SECTION ONE:

The Image of Concentration

"*. . . that they which see not, might see . . .*"
—ST. JOHN, 9:39

When you look at something, LOOK at i

SECTION TWO:

First Try

How Much DO You See?

Study the following four pictures carefully. See HOW
MUCH you can "see," and then write it all down, as
you had actually been watching the scene, and wanted
tell someone about it.

You may write this in any form—narrative, essay
or detailed description—but it will probably be mor
effective if you imagine yourself talking to someone wh
had not seen the old lady, or the gathering of student
or the political meeting, or the three young actresses wai
ing in the wings.

No elaborate instructions are given here about HOW
to write, because the point is to concentrate on WHA
and HOW MUCH you have to say, as a result of obser
vation.

SECTION THREE:

The Power of Observation

All the pictures in this section are in a sense puzzle pictures, for there is something special about each one, which has to be discovered by sharp observation. For the student, the difficulty varies: in some cases, it is nearly impossible to tell what the photographer was trying to convey; whereas in others, perceptive study will reveal what is happening.

In the former instances, write your defense of an interpretation, with details from the picture to uphold what you believe. Where the "secret" can be determined, write about "it" in relation to the rest of the picture.

These pictures involve assignments in what is strictly called "the power of observation." You are to look for a meaning you do not know at first, but which may be there to be discovered, if you can "see" the right things and understand their relationships. Unlike later assignments, you are still not going to be held to a particular kind of writing: the emphasis here again is on pure subject matter—WHAT have you found to say?

Although the answer may be found in details, you should also listen to hunches, since the truth may be found in what you "feel."

In many cases, those who never find anything "special" in these pictures have to be told. Their reply is usually, "Why, I never even noticed that!" The whole philosophy of this book is that bad work, in school and out, is generally the result of the things you "didn't even notice."

ON YOUR OWN

Can you remember a person, a situation, or a scen
that at first you did not understand, but that later, throug
your own searching or someone's explanation, becam
clear?

Here is the basis for a good composition. On a
experimental basis, try writing it in three parts:

1. A description of the subject matter, and a clea
   account of what puzzled you.
2. An explanation of the answer.
3. The effect of the discovery on you.

Or, you might write an explanation of why you di
not or could not see the answer in the beginning. Wha
details did you miss? What relationships did you fail t
notice? What ideas occurred to you that were wrong?

SECTION FOUR:

The Art of Inventing Titles

. . . in a Few Words

A good title is brief and striking; it sums up directly or by suggestion, the most important idea or feeling or action in a picture, just as it does for a painting, a motion picture, or a book.

As you study the following photographs, write single words as they occur to you. Then pick the most accurate and appropriate one as a title.

Next, try the same exercise with phrases of four or five words.

If nothing appears which seems satisfactory, try writing very short sentences that sum up the essence of the picture. This may be done directly: "The photographer was trying to communicate . . ."; or indirectly: "The doctor looked as if he wondered whether it was worth continuing." From such sentences you may find a suitable title.

One rather special way of finding a title is to sum up in very abstract words what you think the picture, even though it is very specific, suggests about general human experience. This is the hardest to do well, and the easiest to do badly; therefore it is good practice. Are any of the following effective?

| Endless Infinity | The Way Things Are |
| In a Trance | "To Be or Not to Be" |

When you compare your own efforts with others, ask

Which words are the most precise?
Which title makes you say: "There . . . that's got it."
Which shows the most inaccurate observation?
Which is too plain and obvious?
Which one makes you see something you missed at first?

SECTION FIVE:

The Art of Comparison

Likenesses Are the Common Denominator

A small mind sees only differences,
a great mind: similarities.

Here, the specific theme is likeness, but the general idea is still the same: students write badly because they see and think badly.

To cure the patient, many educators attack the symptoms instead of the cause. They red-pencil the punctuation and skip the mind that made the punctuation—a mind that has to be trained to take in more than one thing at a time.

The sooner students begin to notice similarities, the sooner their writing will become more interesting, just as "She was on the beach in her baiting suit" is a more interesting sentence than "She wore a good-looking bathing suit." Furthermore, as students see what things are like, they will begin to have more to say; and this is a vital matter, for much of their difficulty in college is not being able to write as much as teachers demand.

Also, developing the habit of looking for likeness may produce unusual and significant ideas, especially when the first things noticed are the differences. These are obvious, as in the first two pictures. Go beyond the superficial differences, behind them, and through them . . . and search for the kinds of similarity that do not appear at first glance.

Many of the pictures here have been selected in pairs, with common denominators, and these should be observed before any writing is done. Compare all things, tangible and intangible: motion, dress, features, forms, and relationships. Then write out complete comparisons focusing on a single idea that shows the two pictures as variations on a similar theme.

Do not wander aimlessly back and forth between the photographs; organize your thoughts and observations, so that you can see them as connected strings of material.

Before you write anything about the first two pictures, study the following two compositions. Analyz them from the point of view of these questions: Wh is the similarity described? Is it interesting, dramati intelligent? How well is it developed, by details and explanation? Which essay is better, and why?

The Cool Thing to Do

Why do girls go frantic at the sight of a singin star? Why do they dress wildly and wear signs pro claiming their admiration for him? Why do the shriek with joy, pressing forward to talk with him touch him, or get his autograph? It is most likel that their only reason for acting like this is that the wish to be popular with their other teenage friend They think that other girls will like them becaus they have met Tommy Sands, or another singer. Fo the same reason, they feel boys will think they ar sharp and ask for dates.

For much the same reasons, the Princeton students were probably compelled to go to the football game. They must comply with the collegiate style of dress—trench coat and sports-car hat. Like the girls, they are at the game because it is "the" thing to do. If they had not come they would be called grinds or finks, and called down for lack of spirit. These are just small examples of the way our society forces people unwillingly into doing what is "the cool thing to do."

Realization

The picture of the teenage girls watching their singing idol appear and the picture of the spectators at the football game are both pictures of people about to have a thrilling experience. The girls have just seen their singing idol appear, they are surging toward him trying to get near him and get his autograph. The spectators at the football game have just seen a back pop clear of the line and break into the secondary. They are just getting to their feet ready to mightily cheer the brilliant run.

One important similarity between these pictures is that both were taken the split second the event occurred. The back was just breaking away and the star had just appeared when the photographer clicked the camera. Both the spectators and the girls had waited expectantly for a long time for this moment. They are oblivious to everything around them; they are devoting their complete concentration to one man. Their eyes best express their attitude of hope, wonder, and amazement. They are opened wide to absorb the whole scene, and imprint it, like a stamp, on their minds. This intense concentration is due to the realization that this was what they were waiting to see. The excitement floods over them like a wave and this excitement is what binds the two crowds together.

ON YOUR OWN

1. Write a description of two things that are clea[r]
   similar. "Things" may mean objects, buildings, [ac]
   tions, people, scenery—anything where the rese[m]
   blance is striking.
2. Find a similarity between two things that few peo[ple]
   would ever think of comparing. Write a descripti[on]
   and explanation so that, despite obvious differenc[es]
   the reader is impressed not only by the likeness, b[ut]
   by its importance.
3. Explain the most interesting similarity you have ev[er]
   heard about, or read about.
4. Think of a commonly accepted similarity which y[ou]
   consider false. Explain why it is unconvincing, [or]
   superficial.
5. Describe the fundamental similarity between tw[o]
   good friends; or—and this would be a real test[—]
   between a good friend and an enemy.
6. Describe the similarity between a child and an adu[lt]

SECTION SIX:

Contrast

"THAT's what makes the big difference!"

The most difficult part of this assignment is choosing important contrasts. It is easy to write about differences that are obvious and silly; but to describe those that "really mean something"—that is another matter.

The first point to remember is that it does not mean much to discuss differences that do not begin in similarities. In the first picture, for example, it is obvious that the subjects, the shapes, and the complexions are different.

But it is more significant to notice how the three figures do the same thing differently. Observe the expressions on the three faces, the suggestions of motion, and the spirit of the two girls as against the chimp. These contrasts would produce a composition of real interest and if done well, of genuine entertainment.

Or, in the case of the next two pictures, it is easy to see that the two dogs present an almost entirely different appearance. This, however, is not so important or striking as the reasons why these differences exist. Even more important as a subject for writing would be a discussion of certain similarities as background for contrasts.

Following the pictures of the setter and the greyhound are two examples of how students developed contrasts, one weak, the other strong. Before writing your own, analyze the reasons why one is better, especially in the choice of material.

John and Fido

John was always an ambitious dog. He would work hard for his food by barking, digging holes in the yard, and playing with the children. When his master took pictures of John he would sit up and look as if he was ready to snap up a dog biscuit.

John's housemate on the other hand was more of a quiet dog. Fido would spend his days sleeping or wandering about the house. Frequently he would sleep in a chair with his shoulder pressed against the arm. Fido enjoyed life, for he knew he didn't have to work for his food.

John's and Fido's master was very fond of his dogs. He took their pictures many times and showed them to his friends. Most everybody thought that Fido was much older than John, because Fido looked so quiet and without ambition. But it turned out that Fido was younger than John; for when John died Fido lived another seven years before he too gave up the ghost.

Dogs and People

Dogs can resemble people in many ways. The pictures of the greyhound and the setter typify this resemblance.

The greyhound is the lean, athletic type of dog, always on the go. If he were human he would have a deep sun-tan from playing a great deal of tennis without his shirt. His leanness does not stem from the fact that he does not eat a great deal; quite to the contrary he eats all he can get, but still stays thin because he is always so active. He is quite healthy, and never refuses a game or challenge. He is so eager for exercise that when there is no one around to compete with he either competes against himself or goes out looking for a challenge. He is adept at every type of skill requiring great coordination or speed: scuba diving, surfing, skiing, tennis, or balancing on a bongo board, and he never gets enough of any of these activities. The look on his face best typifies his attitude: he is eager, so eager his tongue hangs out in anticipation of new adventures.

The setter, the greyhound's critic, is of a somewhat different nature. He is the more dignified and demure of the two. He frowns with disfavor on his energetic colleague. If he were human he would wear tweed, smoke a pipe, have impeccable manners, and engage in important philosophical discussions that would not interest Greyhound in the least. When Greyhound goes scuba diving, Mr. Setter stays home and reads about the state of the world. When Greyhound is playing tennis, Mr. Setter is going to the opera. When Greyhound is balancing on a bongo board, Mr. Setter is in the art gallery. He is concerned with life and the world situation, and was greatly disappointed that he was not chosen to be put up in Space (though he did step forward to serve his country, he was rejected for physical reasons; Greyhound got the job because of his excellent physical condition). He is indignant at times that Greyhound does not take life a bit more seriously but he forgives Greyhound's foolish ways. Greyhound, with much more insight than you would expect, also forgives his.

ON YOUR OWN

What is the most striking difference you ever no ticed between two people, two places, two houses, tw kinds of clothing, two ways of doing the same thing?

Explain the essential nature of this difference b relating to a point of similarity.

Conclude the composition by explaining why thi difference is important.

Also, try these exercises:

1. Contrast a popular and an unpopular student.
2. Contrast your mother and father.
3. Contrast two brothers, or sisters, or cousins.
4. Contrast an athlete and a nonathlete, or an athlet who is only an athlete and one who is also a goo student.

SECTION SEVEN:

Word-Pictures

"What a wonderful thing is metaphor!"
—CHRISTOPHER FRY

There is another version of thinking by comparison: seeing in simile and metaphor.

Most people look at one thing, and see it as just that one thing: they do not instinctively notice resemblances. As they watch an athlete, or a snowstorm, or a girl's face, or a sunset, they are not reminded of anything else. Or if they are, the comparison rarely appears in their writing or their conversation.

Such "double vision" is usually the result of long training in the use of the eye and the mind, and the other senses. It does not come quickly or nonchalantly, except in genius.

This section focuses on the ability to see what things "are like," and to express that likeness in simile and metaphor. Emphasis, also, will be placed on appropriate comparison. The word "appropriate" is important, for students, when asked to find similarities, generally make bizarre comparisons; and they are not usually conscious of their grotesque imagos.

Try to perceive the spirit of your analogies, so that there is no wild conflict between what you see and what you are reminded of. A superficially clever, but very bad metaphor will illustrate this clash of feeling:

The leaves were lipsticked with autumn.

There may be some similarity of color here, but everything else is wrong, especially the clanking sound of "lipsticked." Nature is honest; lipstick is commercial —nature is natural; lipstick is artificial. In this instance, nature is not funny, but the comparison is almost a joke.

On page 31 you studied the picture of a country doctor, and then tried to compose a title. The same picture will be used here, as the subject of metaphor. First consider the following attempts. Which are accurate? Which inappropriate? Which silly, or clumsy?

He looks like a cop who has seen his first hit-and-run fatality.

A great despair clutches his spirit.

Reality has finally caught up with him.

His eyes are looking into the darkened area of destiny.

. . . a cigarette and a cup of coffee held by hands of mercy.

He's a boxer resting before getting back into the next fight.

The life of the patient, who has just undergone the operation, flutters like a curtain in the wind.

Time falls like the ashes of the cigarette, so slowly.

His tiredness is etched on his face.

If he doesn't watch out, he'll have ashes in his coffee.

His steady hands grip the cigarette and coffee unconsciously in the curtain of fatigue.

His hands held the saucer and cigarette as if they were surgical instruments.

The coffee had become tepid as old dishwater while cigarette ashes formed stagnant clots in the black puddle.

The following student metaphors will give you genuine test of your imagination, for they are to associated with a peculiar picture. Physical similarity less important than imaginative, or spiritual, because th point of the picture is not what was photographed, b what is suggested by what was photographed.

Study these analogies, and then compare them wit the picture on the following page.

1. It is a dead face.
2. This picture does not portray any feeling exce conformity to a mold.
3. The heavy makeup and glassy stare of his eyes . .
4. This is a picture of martyrdom.
5. It is a giant paradox: part of the bust is huma part is made of clay.
6. It has an indignant and haughty expression, lik a goddess frowning down on the weaknesses (mankind.
7. The photographer was probably very cynic. about mankind, and she was trying to bring o the bleakness of human existence.
8. A skin of white marble . . . and the aimless sta of eyes in death.
9. This face reminds me of men I know back hom from the woods in Vermont, whose weathe beaten, leathery countenances show no feelin, and only their eyes express the workings of the keen minds.
10. These are the icy stare, the hard nose, and th tightly shut mouth of a ruthless, daring empero
11. The makeup makes his face as rough as a poorl plastered wall.

A good metaphor will always be visually sharp, and mysteriously imaginative. It will, almost always, be something of a surprise, too. One of the best tests to apply is the statement: "Why, I never thought of that before." If you can say this, and at the same time be impressed with the appropriateness of the similarity, then the metaphor is good. Finally, a metaphor should suggest more than it actually states, unlike the directions on a medicine bottle.

Apply these standards to the following professional examples:

1. "His face was a muscle playground, ugly, square and active—rippling with little spasms that might have been taken for thought."—John Hersey.

2. ". . . the trees were as bright as a shower of broken glass."—Christopher Fry.

3. "A lie can travel around the world and back again while the truth is lacing up its boots."—Mark Twain.

4. "Along the platform the patient sheep huddled together in thick clusters, their obedient toes upon the white lines painted on the floor. There was a roaring in the bowels of the earth, and a train, like a lighted dragon, ran out of the cave, its voracious body swollen with heads and shoulders and uplifted arms."—A. P. Herbert.

5. "The slow smokeless burning of decay."—Robert Frost.

6. "The great enemy of clear language is insincerity. When there is a gap between one's real and one's declared aims, one turns as it were instinctively to long words and exhausted idioms, like a cuttlefish squirting out ink."—George Orwell.

7. "To stumble in the spotlight never did anybody any good, and if the man who falls happens to be nineteen years old he may get an ego bruise which will leave him permanently tender."—Heywood Broun.

8. "Trust thyself: every heart vibrates to that iron string."—Ralph Waldo Emerson.

9. "Conversation in the feminine language consists of language rapidly vibrating or oscillating between two persons."—Christopher Morley.

10. "Modern colleges keep books like ledgers in which the student is reduced to credits, merits, hours per week, and weeks per year. They can fill him out in five minutes as sixty percent Christian, forty-five percent normal, assiduity guaranteed up to fourteen hours a day—saturation point—and intelligence tested five times under pressure and never burst."—Stephen Leacock.

ON YOUR OWN

Over a period of several weeks, write a dozen or so sentences identifying things which you know are unfamiliar to your classmates: actions, buildings, accidents, clothes, noises, shapes, people, etc.

The word "identify" has been used here, instead of "describe," to focus your attention more sharply on the idea of conveying the essence of what you see: that is, the most important part of anything that tells what it really "is."

Also, this time, in contrast to writing directly, which is what you do most of the time, write each sentence with a metaphor that suggests what a thing is—its identification—by showing what it is like.

As another kind of assignment on this section, you might compare the quotations on the "Toward a More Picturesque Speech" page of the *Reader's Digest* with the metaphors on pages 66 and 67 of this book. Which are more accurate, appropriate, effective, colorful, exciting, suggestive?

SECTION EIGHT:

Emphasis

"Do you see what I see?"

One of the most difficult and important aspects of writing is emphasis, saying something so that it stands out—like a lighted match on a blacked-out stage. Student writing is often weak because the good ideas have been poorly, vaguely, or wrongly emphasized, so that they do not appear to be more important than others.

One main problem is that students fail to decide beforehand, on the basis of observation and thought, what should be stressed. If they do make a strong case, it is often a matter of luck.

Study the following pictures and decide what is the most vital thing to say about each one. Then write a page or so leading up to the point. Arrange your details so that they all contribute to the main point, and be careful what you place just before the final statement.

In the process of writing the whole composition, practice on individual sentences, arranging the material in them so that one idea stands out.

The word "arrange" here refers primarily to the position in the sentence. English is basically a language of position, so that it makes a great difference WHERE

put your biggest ideas, and HOW you arrange the
s around them.

As a general rule for all writing—sentence, para-
h, and whole composition—the end is the position of
test importance, and the beginning the next. Finally,
emphasize a rule by breaking it, the weakest con-
uting ideas should go in the middle.

Study the placement of ideas and images in the fol-
ing composition written about the picture on page 75.

e Sand

Billions of them are heaped up in great, white,
dry mounds. They are jammed together, successively
more compressed by others like them, until at the
bottom of the mound the pressures exerted by each
can only be measured in thousands of pounds per
square inch. Still they are not crushed. Each particle
of sand remains whole and intact, as if it were in-
divisible.

Those near the surface are whipped into space by
pretentious blasts of wind and are carried for miles,
constantly colliding with one another at frenzied
velocities. They rebound erratically, crashing through
the sea of mayhem that surrounds them, which is
themselves. But they are not broken.

Finally they come to rest again heaped one upon
another. They are intimate, especially those deeply
buried, but they don't recognize one another. For
they are all the same, and always have been, and
always will be.

A plane falls, a thirsty man crawls, a wind blows,
and they are in the air. They bury the plane and
stifle the man, but they are not moved except by the
merciless currents that jostle them aloft. The plane
and the man are gone, and only a few of them know
to where. But they will never tell, for they are like
the others. They will continue to mutely shift, slide,
and collide as they always have and. always will.

ON YOUR OWN

Out of your memory, select a scene in which a great many things happen at the same time:

1. The minutes right after a great athletic victory.
2. The results of an unpopular announcement before a crowd.
3. Confusion at home when several children all want the same thing at once.
4. The first few minutes after any kind of accident.
5. A large fight.

Write an account of this happening in which, though you mention many things, you place 'them and express them so that they all appear less important than one outstanding part of the whole situation.

"Where were you?"

Students often hear their work criticized for lack of coherence, poor organization, and weak unity.

Though these are all good critical terms, the expression "point of view" will be used here, since it emphasizes the problem more acutely.

Look at one of your compositions as a purely physical matter: "Where was I standing in relation to what I saw?" This is one meaning of "point of view." Then, study your work with a different question: "What difference did the fact that I am a particular kind of person make in what I said?" These two queries are the foundation of control over point of view, since the organization, or the form, of a piece of writing is governed by the relationship between writer and subject matter.

For each picture, imagine you are a particular person observing the scene from a particular place, and that you have definite ideas about the time, the atmosphere, the people, and the conflicts. Then write these observations from the point of view of the character you imagine yourself to be.

For the first one, for example, which was taken at a ceremonial parade in Vienna, imagine you are (1) in the parade looking at the audience, (2) the officer with the sneer, (3) a policeman watching for trouble, (4) a spy from a rival government, (5) or an American tourist looking through a zoom lens.

Judge your writing by asking whether your words are those your imagined character would be likely to use, and whether expressions in one part of the composition contradict feelings, ideas, and attitudes expressed in another.

Here are two different attempts by the same student to write from a specific point of view about the first picture. Is one any more controlled than the other? Why?

"Twenty Years After"

I remember the day of the big parade. Thousands of people turned out to view a military show of might put on by the People's Republic. As military police, our job was to retain the crowd. We stood, arms linked, with a line of young schoolchildren in front of us. The youngsters were amazed and happy during the parade. Yet the little boy in front of me never smiled. His countenance displayed a frown. It was almost as if he knew, as I knew, that this parade marked the end of the Austria we had known. There was no more German People's Republic, no more war triumphs, no life without the party. Communism was our new way of life. The old ways and existence were over. This was to be our future.

As I look back, I remember a big parade when I was ten. The military strength exhibited then impressed me tremendously. All the other children my age were giggling with excitement and wonder. If I remember correctly, I was quiet. I looked up into the scowling face of the man in uniform behind me. He was frowning. As I think back now, his face seemed to portray the feelings of the adults. Disillusioned, they were seeing the end of their old way of life. I was seeing the beginning of my new life. And yet, as children often do, I mimicked the man, wearing a frown as the tanks and marching men passed. How foolish I was then. The Party is the only way of life. The Republic is life. There is nothing old, only the new.

ON YOUR OWN

The next time you see anyone in a fight or an argument, stop and observe—with the idea, later, that y[ou]
will retell what happened from the point of view of o[ne]
of the people involved.

It will be good practice, while the battle is on, [to]
decide which one you have the least sympathy for, a[nd]
then watch him (or her) very closely. When you wr[ite]
try to put yourself in the position of the antagonist.

SECTION TEN:

Seeing an Idea

"Do you know what it all means?"

In every assignment so far presented, one of th
great problems of writing and thinking has been implied
the conflict between the abstract and the concrete, be
tween the general and the specific.

Many failures are primarily failures in this area
failures in coping with abstractions, failing to be SPE
CIFIC. Most of the time, students do not realize tha
they are dealing with abstractions, and therefore have n
idea why their writing is weak.

This section focuses sharply on this difficulty. Th
compositions are assigned on abstract ideas as suggeste
by the pictures; and the development of each paper mus
include references to the concrete realities actually photo
graphed.

What an idea is, really, is a collection—an abstrac
collection—of concrete details. Democracy, for example
is an idea, a general form of government, an abstrac
theory, which in operation is made up of thousands o
individual, specific actions. Without these actions, ther
is nothing but a theory, which looks very good in th
dictionary. Precisely the same thing is true of such ab
stractions as terror, love, thought, education, corruptions
and rhythm. These are words; and words are alway
abstractions. Try and catch one.

Study the following pictures and decide on one gen
eral idea, or thought, or feeling suggested by details i
the picture. One way of doing the composition is very
direct: expressing the idea and then illustrating it, almos
as if you were trying to prove it. The other is indirect
describing selected details so precisely and suggestivel
that no reader can miss the idea, even though it is no
stated.

The composition across the page shows how on
student developed an idea about the first picture. Almos
every problem in student writing is illustrated here, from
punctuation to choice of material.

A boy is out walking with a knapsack strapped to his back. He is thinking that he is an explorer; a discoverer; the first person ever to travel "these parts." This is a game played by children in every country, and though the surroundings change, the excitement never does. This boy is universal.

The thing that sets this one particular boy apart from all the rest, is his strange surroundings. He is walking down a large set of stairs leading toward a group of buildings which have been bombed and are nearly completely demolished. Only concrete shells of their original forms remain, some large piles of rubble, and great gaping holes in the buildings, which add to the hollow and empty feeling. Many wild clumps of bushes, lining the stairs, fail to add any feeling of life.

The only living thing in the picture is the small boy. He is a contrast to the rest of the picture. He is in surroundings which are old and dead. The boy is young and alive. The buildings are bleak and harsh. The boy is soft.

There is a more important contrast in this picture, though: it is the one between what came before the picture was taken, and what is to come after it. The buildings show what came before. That was a generation that produced nothing but the war which destroyed the buildings. The boy signifies hope for what is to come. He is young, and has a chance to produce something out of his life which is creative, rather than the destructive things his parents produced. The boy signifies the hope of all mankind in their children. All people want their children to grow up with a better chance to achieve more than they themselves had. This boy, living as he does in the midst of ruins and death, and acting the same way any child might, by "exploring" the ruins, symbolizes these desires of mankind.

ON YOUR OWN

Take time off and observe a crowd or a group
people in action: at a meeting, a game, a restaurant,
a bull session . . . something like that.

Sit still, listen, and observe sounds, gestures, wor
facial expressions, physical relationships, and attitu
between individuals: conflict, perhaps, or similarities.

Afterward, try to abstract from all these details
general meaning—an idea—about the way these peo
were behaving.

Write a fully developed paragraph explaining a
describing your conclusion about what was going on. U
as many details as possible from the scene, and expr
the whole paragraph as if you were trying to commu
cate to someone who wasn't there.

Do the same thing by using the details, but nev
stating the general idea, or the abstraction, direct
Choose just the right things to make your reader feel t
impression.

SECTION ELEVEN:

Conflict

No Contest? No Interest!

No short story, novel, essay, poem, or play would successful without conflict. In fact, every work of liter art is based on opponents and opposition.

Only one student in a hundred, however, wr about conflict observed in actual life. Students pr "nice" subjects, or subjects so abstract that it is easy avoid tension, like "Friendship," "Education," or " Philosophy."

Many people run away from conflict. Or perh they simply do not see conflict because they have ne learned to look for it, except in athletic contests. (tainly they are surprised when conflict is required what they write.

The pictures in this section are aimed at a sea for conflict, so that eventually students will have, re in mind, the kind of basic material that makes for g writing. Every one of these pictures reveals confl Some dramatize sharp physical opposition, some sugg it subtly; some reveal contrasts in line, idea, force, shape; and some show a tight tension that does not pear in motion, but in a frozen moment of inner strug

1. Write one sentence that conveys a physical c flict dramatically, in any one picture.
2. Write one suggesting inner conflict.
3. Explain how one detail emphasizes a major c flict, or tension.

4. Write a full paragraph describing the atmosphere of tension captured in a picture.
5. Convey the conflicting forces through a metaphor. What is the conflict "like"?
6. Imagine the thoughts of one character involved in the struggle.

You have already done exercises involving problems emphasis and point of view. In the following student mposition, written about the situation pictured on page , these problems appear again as a young writer tries develop the idea of conflict. Can you explain where s student becomes confused in emphasis, and also es control of a coherent point of view?

pentant

As I sat behind the table checking the refugee's identification I noticed how different this woman was from all the other people. She was dressed in German field grays. She said her boy friend had given them to her because clothes were so hard to get at the end of the war. Now her home had been destroyed, her friends and family killed, and she had nowhere to go.

Most of the other refugees had been recently released from German prison camps, and the guards were Free French with their typical berets. The war had so hardened most that they displayed no emotion toward the woman.

One buxom woman though displayed a violent hatred toward the German. I could understand the woman's hatred—she'd just been released from prison last week, and yesterday she'd learned that her whole family had been killed. I still felt sorry for the German woman who was receiving the butt of the hatred, for now she looked so repentant and sorry. I wondered how sorry the German woman would have looked if they had won the war.

ON YOUR OWN

1. Narrate a series of actions between two people who are obviously in conflict: boy–girl, child–parent, student–teacher, athlete–referee, performer–heckler. Don't use any dialogue; try to make the opponents move in relation to each other so that it is clear that they want different things, and that for some time these desires are opposed.
2. Do the same thing with dialogue.
3. Describe a series of actions between a man and a thing he cannot "push around."
4. Describe a very silly conflict between two people.
5. Narrate a difficult scene between one person and a group who want him to keep quiet.

To hold a mirror up to human nature

One of the most powerful forces in human existen is character. It is so strong that every writer througho literary history has placed more emphasis on charact than any other element. Students are made constant aware of this fact as they study stories, novels, and play They are continually asked to consider the nature of th character, the thoughts of that one, the motives another, and the way one individual is related to anothe

In actual life, the importance of character and pe sonality is so great that in the settling of human co flict, one of the first things considered is not just wh a particular man or woman did, but how and why he d it. This involves the difficult task of figuring out wh goes on in the mind, in the emotions, and in the instinc

There are various ways of discovering such trut but one of the most significant is the study of facial e pressions, gestures, tones of voice, and movements of th body. These are the outward signs of thought and fee ing, and though they may be misleading, they are s often right that they cannot be ignored. In the best sens of the word, no one can be called "educated" until he h. learned, by reading these signs, to observe some of th great truths of character.

Such a study of character is justified by a fund. mental moral principle: the understanding of oth people. It is much like the process of analyzing chara ters in books, and this way of thinking can be transferre to actual life. Every good professional writer masters th skill before he writes anything worth reading.

The pictures in this section have been selected b cause they reveal character through expression, gestur

action. Look carefully at the curve of a mouth, the
[ ]t of an eye, the lines of a face, the gesture of a
[ ]d, the posture of a whole body. What do all these de-
[ ]s suggest about the individual? What traits would you
[ ]ect to find in such people? What would you expect
[ ]m to do in a conflict?

It may occur to you that these pictures show only
[ ] brief glimpse of character. This is true. You will
[ ]lize only a limited understanding from these photo-
[ ]phs. Yet this limited perception is important and real-
[ ]c, for it is very like the limited perceptions you gain
[ ]m actual observation.

In many of these pictures, the subject did not know
[ ] was being photographed, with the result that there is
[ ] doubt about the genuineness of the emotion. Even in
[ ] posed pictures, there is virtue in discovering what
[ ]e the subject was trying to play, what "image" he was
[ ]jecting.

When discussing friends, most of us can say noth-
[ ]g more than "He's a nice guy," or "What a dope!" or
[ ]tupid!" We don't see enough to say "He's unselfish,"
[ ]"She's shy," or "Don't be intolerant."

Close study of these pictures will yield many exer-
[ ]es. Here is a good place to do whole compositions:
[ ]scribe in unified form the meaning of relationships in
[ ] group, or the way one person is thinking. Another
[ ]od exercise is hunting for single words that best cap-
[ ]re the meaning of an expression. Or, try a metaphor to
[ ]ggest what you see under the surface.

Finally, here is a chance to consider connotations.
[ ]though the dictionary may say the meaning is right,
[ ] sound of a word may be inappropriate, or its sug-
[ ]stions may conflict with something in the picture. One
[ ]st is fairly reliable: if your language is greeted with a
[ ]wl of laughter, you may be sure something is wrong,
[ ]her with your vision, or your language. Here are a
[ ]w attempts to analyze the character of the man on the
[ ]llowing page. Try your own description. Then, charac-
[ ]rize the people in the remaining pictures in this section.

1. I see a young Negro worker sitting in a darkened theater, excessively tired from a taxing day's work, meditating while awaiting the start of the evening performance.
2. I saw a curious Negro with baggy trousers sitting alone in a theater, his eyes focused on some very interesting sight.
3. In the front of a filthy deteriorated theater sat a tired Negro with well-used dusty clothing.
4. I see the utter desolation, loneliness, and solitude of the Negro race as portrayed by the lone black man sitting by himself in the tattered theater.
5. What I see is a desolate, poorly treated Negro sitting in his part of a segregated theater.
6. Sitting casually in a virtually empty theater is a Negro dressed in seedy clothes staring downward at nothing.
7. ... one lonely Negro sitting slouched in one of the many seats, his large white eyes piercing the gloom and eery dark.
8. I saw a perfect example of the sadness of the discrimination which has plagued our country.
9. He was sitting slouched in a chair looking beady-eyed at the movie screen.
10. ... a look of complete hopelessness. ...
11. ... a very lonesome-looking Negro with his leg crossed, wearing sloppy old clothes, staring at a boy walking across the stage.
12. As I walked into the theater I saw, in the front row, a grubby decrepit hobo-type Negro with a somewhat guilty and preoccupied look on his face as though he was supposed to be working and his employer walked in.
13. ... he looked as though he'd lost his last friend.
14. ... a very dejected figure ... sitting all alone in the front row, with no one else in the whole theater. ..

ON YOUR OWN

There are several ways to tell about a person's character.

One is to come right out and say what he is, and then show how these traits appear in action.

Another is not to make any direct statements—"He was so selfish that he couldn't . . ."—but to describe individual reactions so clearly that the reader can't miss.

A third approach is to imagine what the person is thinking about, and then write out these thoughts so realistically that the reader will understand the person he is "observing."

Another way—a variation—is to narrate a dialogue, thus suggesting the nature of the person.

Choose one of these, or perhaps a combination, and write two or three pages about someone you know, trying to make the reader sense how this person feels, thinks, acts, and looks. Your objective is really to make your subject so clear that the reader can guess what he would do in another situation.

SECTION THIRTEEN:

Dialogue

"That sounds just like him"

For the following pictures, write a page or two of conversation, as you imagine it might have happened.

This is a logical result of the previous section, since conversation depends on character, as affected by situation.

Before writing, imagine who these people are, what they are probably thinking under the circumstances, what they are feeling, and what their voices would sound like. Seek also for a natural connection between their words and their actions.

Another approach is to imagine the nature of the conflict these people are involved in, and then develop dialogue that could be caused by the difficulty. Or, as a variation, in the case of the first picture, write dialogue that shows a contrast between the children and the scenery.

The most important thing is to choose language appropriate to the speaker, so that the reader "sees" what he may be thinking.

Finally, make the conversation lead up to a climax, to a positive conclusion from what has been said. The reader should finish with the feeling that the subject is over, at least for the time being, and that the next bit of talk will be about something else.

ON YOUR OWN

What is the most memorable conversation you heard?

Re-create it as if it were a scene from a play, after each speech put in parenthesis a concise indica of how the words should be said, and how the spea might act accordingly.

One obvious way to do this is to remember an a ment. But, also, see if you can do a scene in which m ideas and feelings were suggested or hinted at, ra than laid on thick.

SECTION FOURTEEN:

A Good Story

What Happened?

To tell a story well demands much understandi
and many techniques, and this section does not prete
to tell you all about how it is done: but it can start y
practicing on several of the most important elements
narrative.

The first thing is to study all pictures in each ser
in order to make up your mind about the main idea y
will emphasize. No one should ever begin a story witho
knowing the general purpose that holds all details
gether.

This "main idea" may be a thought, a conclusi
a comment, or a powerful emotion. Ideally, it should
suggested by all the details you use, so that when y
come to the end, you won't have to spell it out direc
in so many words, to the reader's face.

This result depends on selecting the right deta
from each picture, and rejecting others, no matter h
attractive. Your job is to choose only those things th
are important to the main reason you are telling the stor

When you come to the problem of putting your m
terial in order, the main point to remember is that ever
thing should be told in ascending order so that your t
rises up to a point of excitement or humor or revelati

the end. There should be a real contrast in strength between the various parts of your story, especially the beginning and ending.

In stories involving people, pick details to tell what the characters are thinking, even if their mouths are open. Here you will have to use your imagination, to figure out what their faces suggest that they may be thinking, as you did in the section on characterization.

Always, as you are planning and writing, make it clear that every sentence and paragraph adds something definite to the point of the narrative. You should be able to explain just what any given detail actually contributes. Test things by asking continually: "How does this relate to what I have just said?"

At some point in this exercise you should probably write out in so many words what the main idea or purpose is, for this will serve as a guide when you are choosing details; but most important, it will be the basis for what you say at the ending.

One thing you must NOT do is state a moral. It is a completely mistaken idea that a story must have a moral to be any good, and one has only to read a book of great stories to find how untrue this myth is. You can, of course, suggest a moral idea, or give a hint of some sort; but what you should really try to do is give the reader a surprise at the end. This may involve an idea about character, or a line or two of dialogue, or a specific detail of action, or some new thought about the whole sequence.

There are two good tests to apply to an ending, one for yourself, and one for the reader.

Imagine the reader looking up after the last sentence and asking, "Now what is that supposed to mean?" If you can say "It's just that that's the way things are," you have probably written a good ending.

Imagine, however, that the reader has the last word: "Why, I never even noticed that," or "I never thought of that before." If your last sentence makes him say this, you also have a good conclusion.

ON YOUR OWN

Pick a story out of your own experience . . . o
that actually led up through a series of incidents to
climactic and meaningful conclusion.

Arrange the details in ascending order, and the
write the story so photographically that the reader w
be able to "see" what happened as if he had been ther

When you check through the first draft, ask you
self whether you have really SHOWN that the even
happened, not simply SAID that they happened. The d
ferences are revealed in the following paragraphs:

"From the way she acted, it was clear Jackie d
not like the new boy in town."

"Jackie looked over his shoulder and waved fra
tically to another boy in a red convertible.

" 'Huh?' she said vaguely. . . . 'What was it y
were saying?' "

SECTION FIFTEEN:

The Unexpected

The World is Full of Surprises

As you observe what people are doing and saying and what is happening near you, look for surprises, for things you never noticed about things you have seen many times before. Out of such observation comes the best material for good writing. The purpose of this text is to point out not only that good thinking is the result of precise observation, but to dramatize the eventual fusion of the two in creative writing.

The trouble with student subjects is antiquity: the same old things are being written about in the same old ways, like stamp collecting, trips to the seashore, favorite hobbies, and that first date. You can, of course, write about the same old things in your own special way.

For practice, choose the most hackneyed subject you can think of, and write about it from a most unusual point of view. Or, write about a discovery made through unexpected observation.

The following pictures illustrate either extraordinary subject matter—the unexpected—or ordinary subject matter treated in an extraordinary way. Here, the observer looks, stops, and thinks. For each picture, write a full explanation of what the photographer has made you notice, particularly about what might have been a routine subject.

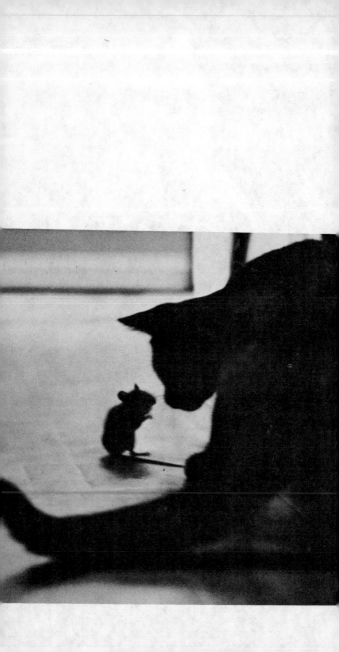

The pictures in this section present a special pr
lem: the use of language to suggest motion. This
difficult because of the contradiction that you will
trying to create a sense of motion with something t
doesn't move—words. Literally, they stand still.

Their meanings, however, do not: and therefore,
must concentrate on finding words whose meanings
active. This is one reason why teachers object to ve
in the passive voice.

Even active verbs can sometimes be ineffecti
verbs like "go," "use," "walk," "move," "act,"

e." Although they do convey some sense of move-
t, it is such a soft and general sense that no strong,
y, memorable impression springs up in the reader's
d. It's better to use words like "race," "poke,"
nce," "slink," "show off," and "snatch" . . . as long
ou don't use too many of them. The virtue of such
ion is that it makes a sharp, clear picture of a specific
ement that is not like a lot of others.

Or you can go further and use phrases and clauses,
other combinations of words which, when read to-
er, convey a sense of motions happening together.

> She sat there, not eating much and keeping a
> sharp eye out for a vacant place on any plate and
> watching the jaws work, and as she sat there, her
> face seemed to smooth itself out and relax with an
> inner happiness the way the face of the chief en-
> gineer does when he goes down to the engine room
> at night and the big wheel is blurred out with its
> speed and the pistons plunge and return and the big
> steel throws are leaping in their perfect orbits like
> a ballet, and the whole place sings and glitters . . .
> and the ship is knocking off twenty-two knots on a
> glassy starlit sea.
> —ROBERT PENN WARREN, *All the King's Men*

Here is another passage, creating a different kind of
ion.

> A stately squadron of snowy geese were riding
> in an adjoining pond, convoying whole fleets of
> ducks: regiments of turkeys were gobbling through
> the farmyard, and guinea fowls were fretting about
> it, like ill-tempered housewives, with their peevish
> discontented cry.

After studying the first picture, write phrases, or com-
e sentences, expressing the motion you see in the
e. Try to think in terms of the particular kind of
ion your words suggest.

ON YOUR OWN

Write a sentence, or a phrase, describing each of the
following motions:

A car skidding.
A basketball going around the rim of the basket, and then
dropping outside (or inside).
A rock-'n'roll guitar player.
A jagged streak of lightning.
Cars on a freeway all going 70 m.p.h.
A car coming at you going too fast.
A girl flirting.
A football player avoiding a tackle.
A fishing rod bending as a fish runs.
An adult spanking a child.
A cop trying to hurry a slow driver.
Someone at a meeting trying to get attention.
The most characteristic gesture of an actor or actress.
The peculiar habit of a friend.
Someone smoking who doesn't know how.
Anybody showing off.
Smoke and flames.
A cat stalking a bird, or a squirrel.
Snow falling.
A water skier swinging out on an arc.

Most of this book is devoted to observation as primary basis of good writing. But the other senses vital, too, as almost all good writing reveals; for gr authors have always worked hard to find the right wo suggesting what they have felt, tasted, or heard.

Most young writers, however, are only dimly aw of sounds, textures, and odors, with the result that th compositions are flat and soft. In narrative especia there is no feeling of reality because the characters are surrounded by sensations.

Unhappily, when young writers do try to use language of the senses, they often produce fake "m pieces" filled with words like "gloomy," "eerie," "f tastic," and "hollow." This corn grows tall because writer was simply shoveling up a pile of words; he not using language to mean something he had actu sensed, or observed.

In this section, the pictures have been chosen beca they show how the world can appeal to the senses. L carefully at the smallest details, and imagine how th might feel, or taste, or smell. Find the most accurate a sensitive—and sensuous—words to communicate what there to be observed and sensed.

In view of students' natural tendency to write p ple prose, assignments for this section should be sho single words, phrases, or brief sentences. Metaphor sho be tried also.

Do not wallow in adjectives, for the experience the senses can be conveyed through nouns and verbs. is especially good practice to work on nouns, for if right one is found, then no adjective is needed.

How would you describe the combined
    taste of doughnuts, hamburger,
    and Coca-Cola?
Do it in one word
      ... or in a phrase
      ... or by a metaphor.
Describe it from the point of view
    of the soldiers, according
    to the expressions on their
    faces.

ON YOUR OWN

Go out and watch somebody eating a mess of swe
in a drugstore, or trying to study for an examination,
making preparations for a date, or reacting in an arg
ment. Try to pick an action that involves more than c
of the five senses.

Write about this little "slice of life" as if you we
trying to imitate Dorothy Parker's picture of Annabel a
Midge which was quoted on page 8. Make the reader sm
the smells, hear the noises, feel the surfaces, observe t
motions, and taste the food.

SECTION EIGHTEEN:

Imagination

To Make a World of Your Own

In Section Three, you studied scenes that were no clear. They either appeared to be something they weren't or they resembled nothing you could recognize. With some of the logic of a detective, and the imagination of a poet you discovered the truth.

For the pictures in this section, the purpose is not to discover the truth—in some cases it is pretty obvious— but to imagine things suggested by the pictures: images ideas, visions, analogies, and, perhaps, something out of this world. The point is not, as in Section Three, to find out what the photographer actually "took," but to make up, to invent, to guess. What you communicate here is not what can be proven, but what you see in your mind's eye.

In other words, never mind "the facts."

If you get stuck, consider the following questions:

What might have caused this "thing"?
Have you ever seen anything like it?
What is it NOT?
What is the spirit of the picture?
What is the essential conflict or contrast?
How are the parts of the picture related?
Invent a scene of which this image could have been a part.
Is an abstract idea suggested?
Why do you think the photographer took the picture?
What is suggested by the shapes and forms?
Write a perfectly silly explanation.

ON YOUR OWN

Think of the most puzzling, ambiguous, bewilderi
thing you've ever seen.

Describe it as clearly as you can from memory, a
then sit back and try to imagine various explanations.

Choose the most likely one, work it out in detail, a
write it down in full.

"He speaks nothing but golden banter."
—WALTER WINCHELL

One of the worst writing faults is triteness. It is al[so]
one of the hardest to erase.

When a student is told that his language is hackneye[d]
he is likely to explode: "How can I help it if I've nev[er]
heard the expression before! How can I avoid clichés if [I]
don't know they're clichés!" (One boy dramatized th[e]
whole difficulty by pronouncing the word "clytcha.")

Some textbooks do provide lists of clichés to mem[-]
orize, but this is a mechanical method. It is far better [to]
attack the problem from the point of view that no one w[ill]
sharpen his language until he sharpens his vision, sin[ce]
accurate, emphatic diction results only from seeing th[e]
world in an accurate, emphatic way. Trite words com[e]
from trite thought; and trite thought is nothing but tri[te]
observation.

People who say "great," "nice," and "fabulous" d[o]
so because they have nothing in their minds but the vag[ue]
pleasurableness suggested by such tired words. To descri[be]
character, for example, with words like "unselfish," "fi[n-]
icky," or "calculating" requires the ability to see the[se]
qualities with the eye and the mind. To see the weath[er]
as "murky" demands a different quality of eyesight fro[m]
the kind that sees "lousy."

The function of this section is to dramatize trite thin[k-]
ing and observation so that students can see for themselv[es]
what they are doing. The point is to match stale languag[e]
against a sharp image.

First, study the picture opposite, and then compa[re]
it with the "composition" on the following page. What[']s
wrong?

Eerie

The night was dark as pitch as a lone, solitar
figure wended its weary way through the pea-sou
fog. The only light showing sort of seeped out fro
a queer-looking old street light next to a railroa
crossing where the crossing guards stuck up in th
air straight as a ramrod. I couldn't see too well be
hind them, but I got a hunch there might be som
thing awfully spastic around. It was all kind of eeri
It gave me the shivers, sort of a creepy, crawly fee
ing. I expect the guy in the picture was soaked to th
skin by the lousy fog, and he was probably trudgin
homeward to get right up next to a cozy little fir

and the cozy little woman, and pour himself some of that beer that made Milwaukee famous. He looks as if he were walking at a snail's pace, like he was kind of groping his way. Except for him, everything looks quiet as anything, and silent as the grave. This spooky atmosphere is highlighted by a funny light shining through a signal-like tower, fanning out flashlight-wise.

ow, write your own description.

To intensify the emptyheaded sound of clichés, a oup of hackneyed expressions are listed below, in conast with original images created by professional writers. he difference between them is a matter of invention.

He tried to snow the girl.	"Marrow stood in front of her flexing his jokes."—John Hersey
That book is really something!	"Reading that book will put your eyebrows on stilts."—Walter Winchell
He talks too much.	"He's a man of a few thousand words."—Samuel Goldwyn.
The audience coughed so much you couldn't hear yourself think.	"The audience strummed their catarrhs."—Alexander Woollcott
It was one of those real cool nights . . . you know what I mean?	"The park is filled with night and fog, The veils are drawn about the world, The drowsy lights along the paths, Are dim and pearled." 　　　　—Sara Teasdale
You jerk!	"You dried neat's tongue, you bull's pizzle, you bolting hutch of beastliness. . . ."—Shakespeare

On the opposite page is a picture of one of the most frightening high-wire acts the world has ever seen. It was staged three thousand feet above the craggy rocks of the Zugspitze on the Austro-Bavarian frontier.

The ordinary tourist, if he saw this act, would probably come home and say, "You should have seen the spine-chilling thing we saw last summer. . . . Boy oh boy!"

There is no doubt about the chills going up one's spine on looking at this picture, but there is also no doubt that the word "spine-chilling" is pretty feeble beside the reality in the photograph. The trouble is not that clichés are wrong; it is that they are old and smooth, and pass through the ear and mind like warm wind. Also, they may cover so many meanings—like "exciting" or "dull"—that they do not convey the particular, individual, special meaning of what actually happened.

It is often said that a picture is worth a thousand words, and it would be dramatic if we always had pictures on hand to help us say what we want. But most of the time we are thrown back on words. The only way to learn to communicate expressively and quickly is to study what you see, and study it intently, until you know what the most important thing is, and what words most exactly describe it.

Make a list of all the clichés you can think of to describe this picture—and what this means is the actual reality in the picture—and then try to write a sentence that not only expresses your observation, but expresses it with originality.

Just for the fun of it, write a long corny description of the picture opposite, imitating the style of the composition written about the first picture in this section.

ON YOUR OWN

Study the following clichés in relation to the pictures indicated. Can you explain now why they sound so silly?

	PAGE
There was this stupid little kid standing there like a jerk.	12
The old lady was pouring tea out of a beat-up old kettle.	17
They were packed in like sardines.	18
The girl on the right looks calm and collected.	20
The kids didn't have a chance.	105
They looked as though they thought they were very big deal.	116
They were a coupla pretty sharp characters.	116
He was one a those high-society types.	117
His face showed the ravages of war.	119
The kids were having a ball.	123
The cat was giving the mouse a hard time.	138
The soldiers were standing there with a real dead-pan look.	163
You coulda heard a pin drop.	166
I couldn't make anything out of it.	172
I'd hate to meet him on a dark night.	173
What a sensational picture!	193

What is the most interesting incident you can remember? Write a page about it, using the worst clichés you can think of. Then do another page, trying to be as accurate and suggestive as you can. Try making up your own expressions, and using usual words in unusual combinations.

Life Can Be Funny

For each of the following pictures,

1. Write a one-word title.
2. ... a phrase.
3. ... the most suitable line of dialogue from one of the characters.
4. ... the most appropriate thought from the mind of one of the characters.
5. Find the most applicable quotation.

Explain an abstract idea suggested by the picture.

Write a brief character sketch of the kind of photographer who would take such a picture.

Explain why you think any of these pictures are obvious, or unexpected.

Suppose you heard someone say, "I don't understand why they print such stuff in magazines." Defend the picture.

Explain the most important comparison or contrast that makes the picture effective.

ON YOUR OWN

From memory, write a description of several scenes that are most similar to those in the preceding section, or most different.

Or, if you can't remember anything appropriate, make up a scene that would resemble one picture. You might approach this from the point of view: A Picture I Would Like to See.

Go back to the first four pictures (pages 17–20)—of the old English woman and her teakettle, of the crowd of students, of Churchill amid applause, and of the three young actresses—and write new compositions based on what you have discovered about the powers of observation.

Then, set these beside the first ones you wrote, and analyze fully what you did differently, both in seeing and writing.

On the basis of this experiment, study the following group of pictures—including the picture story of the little girl card player—and write the most fully developed compositions you can invent.

Consider this final test as both quantitative and qualitative: Did you notice any MORE things, and Did you notice different KINDS of things?

Then, compare these last efforts with some of the student writings that begin on page 204.

The Students Write

About the Pictures

The professional writer develops his art, like profes
sionals in other fields, by studying the successes and fai
ures of other writers, ancient and contemporary. In fac
most writers never write well at all until they know some
thing of the history of literature.

Otherwise, like high-school students, they write i
isolation, perpetrating and perpetuating the mistakes o
others. In a sense, they are like many TV writers, palmin
off as new and good, stories discarded fifty years ago i
the movies.

This principle of continuity should be observed i
education. As young writers are learning diction, ser
tence structure, and choice of material, they ought t
know what their predecessors did, and what their fellov
students are doing now: good writing to see what is pos
sible; bad, to avoid conventional errors.

It would be helpful, for example, both for teache
and student, if a boy in Massachusetts who says, "But
didn't know these were hackneyed words!" could be im
mediately shown compositions from Nevada, Mississipp
Florida, and New York, with the same clichés.

It would be helpful, too, for a teacher trying to cor
vince his students to abandon stories about dope addict
if he could demonstrate how bad a composition can b
when the writer doesn't know what he is talking about.

These are two of the main reasons for concluding thi
book with a collection of students' work based on picture

roughout the text. There is the further point, moreover,
at students may gain good ideas for compositions by
udying the work of other students.

In the following short composition on the picture on
age 17, a ninth-grade student reveals an unusual ability
 observe detail with remarkable accuracy and complete-
ss.

anny's Quaint Appearance

Fanny may be poor, but she is not forlorn as she
prepares her tea. Though she is old and wrinkled,
she stands straight and holds her head high. She may
once have been beautiful with those deep-set eyes and
arched eyebrows. Obviously she has few if any teeth
and will probably eat something like crumpets with
her tea, which she pours from a burned and blistered
kettle into a modest little teapot. Her costume is
unique, with its sweater covered by a figured apron
top and a skirt which seems to be made of burlap,
frugally patched. Since she is taking tea she has
donned her best hat at an offset angle to add color
and life to her costume. This rather interesting hat
is the only expensive-looking thing in the room and
leads you to wonder who gave it to her. Perhaps she
picked it up for sixpence in a Thrift Shop. The torn
wallpaper and old board ceiling, from which most
of the plaster has fallen, are separated by a wide
crack. This is the kind of house where termites like
to work. On the wall hangs a curtain, which hides a
modest window, a calendar, and a picture. The mantel is covered with letters and papers doubtless sent
by her friends and children. The mantel drape is
decorated with a design which may be needlework
done by Fanny in an effort to relieve the drabness of
the room. A metal hood partly covers the fireplace, in
which we see some twigs. We do not need to feel
sorry for Fanny, whose capable hands seem proof
enough that she can take care of herself.

The following essay was written about the thr
women on page 54. Read it and then consider the que
tion at the end.

"To Have and Have Not"

Many humans have a strange and unrelenti
desire to obtain certain elements of life which do n
belong to them. Many people daydream, placi
themselves in famous men's shoes or just pretendi
that they are great athletes or millionaires. Rare
are we satisfied and thankful to have that which b
longs to us and be who we are.

Perhaps this greedy desire stems from the co
petition in life. Some people might think that th
are failures just because they don't have two ca
They are therefore inclined to wish that they had th
second car—and a lot more besides.

Nothing can illustrate this point clearer than t
picture of the two old, wealthy women walking
front of a poor pedestrian. One can see on the c
looker's face, an awed expression.

"How could anyone ever have a coat like dat. G
Whiz, dat's A-1. Look at dem lips and dat ha
"WOW!"

And for many days, even weeks, hence that c
looker will be walking in the same shoes, the sa
coat, her lips smeared in red, her eyes gleaming, a
with the slight smile of wealth on her lips.

Is this interpretation justified?

One of the great arts of writing is invention, making up something that did not exist before. Here is what one student "made up" after studying the two pictures on pages 56–57.

War Lords

We were very confident, of course; the little hick planet was sure to be a pushover. After all, Earth was the most powerful planet in the galaxy; in fact, every one of our soldiers was really an army all by himself. With his flame thrower, space warper, gas bombs, bacteria culture, and small, fifty-megaton, tactical, fusion grenades, the average G.I. could take on a whole village of maybe more than three thousand people and completely wipe it out. Yes, we certainly had a right to be proud of our men: they were the best, bar none!

Well, the invasion, scheduled for the middle of summer, started off perfectly. We made a beachhead on the biggest continent—only the size of Greenland, believe it or not—and it wasn't long before the inhabitants were in full retreat—I guess they hadn't been used to fighting! You should have seen their men—amateurs! Why, they looked more like Sunday picnickers than soldiers: they were loaded down with all sorts of truck—shavers, pans, egg beaters, and the like. It was almost funny watching them die.

Pretty soon, though, even though the top brass were keeping things pretty well under cover, we got the word that something was going wrong. We didn't even need the word from upstairs—you could tell by just counting the men in the squads—plenty more than there should have been were gone. First we tried keeping better guard around the camp, figuring that maybe the enemy was kidnapping our men. It didn't do any good, mostly, I suppose, because it was during the battles that they disappeared—every night there'd be fewer and fewer fellows reporting back.

It took us a long time to figure out what wa going on—I guess we were fooled into thinking tha the enemy was completely helpless. What a bunch c sneaks—they had a secret weapon all along an didn't even let on: every time one of our men tumble into their camps, they just sort of offered him foo told him to take his pack off and relax. Well, yo can see easy enough what this kind of trick woul do—when the guys shed that 250-pound pack, ha a little coffee, and maybe even smiled for the fir: time in six years (we were kinda serious in thos days), they went plumb off their rocker, got so shoo up that they couldn't find their way back to our line and had to stay in those pleasure resorts the enem calls their camps.

Funny thing, though, us, the most powerful worl in the universe, we had to leave on account of all ou troops disappearing—yes, sir, just about all of ther got trapped. We ain't ever been able to take tha world since, neither. We don't even dare go near 'e —the dirty hick amateurs!

The following dialogue was written about the political parade pictured on pages 72–73.

Wendell Willkie and John Versus Emma

"It's sort of exciting having the presidential nominee riding through our town. Don't you think so, Emma? He looks so distinguished riding in that handsome black car with a chauffeur and all."

"I'll tell you what I think, John. I think you need new glasses. That man's about as distinguished as a drunken salesman. Look at how his eyes bag out of his head! And look at that tie! There must be every color in the world swimming in that tie. Let me tell you, John; I wouldn't vote for that . . ."

"Oh, shut up, Emma. You know you're just trying to put on an act. You're as excited as anyone. Doesn't it kinda do something to you to see all those American flags. I'll bet there's four of 'em on every post in town.

"Hey! Look . . . he's wavin' to us, Emma. God! He's standing right up and waving to us. I'm going to vote for him, Emma. How about you?"

"I think it's disgraceful the way the people in this town act. Look at them, screaming, and hollering and behaving like a bunch of kids. I can't see but two jackets in the whole crowd."

"Oh, for goodness' sakes, Emma. It's ninety degrees. Look at all those black cars. I wonder what those big cardboard numbers are for: the ones on the windshields."

"Let's go back to the farm, John."

The following composition was written about the three Germans pictured on page 114. In addition to the usual problems—mechanics, diction, sentence structure, etc.—study the organization of the essay as a whole. From the point of view of placement of subjects, how has the student changed the emphasis from the picture?

War

In this photograph I see three men expressing their emotions of the war without ever speaking a word.

The boy seems new to the brutality of war and sits, silently staring into his cup. However, the signs of war are already present in the empty look in his eyes. I don't think he has grasped the reality of war, but he has probably had his first glimpse of the useless slaughter that surrounds him. He is probably wondering how he became engulfed in the nightmare of war.

The soldier without a shirt has probably seen many massacres. He has the look of a man who knows what it is to gore an enemy soldier for no other reason than that he is just "the enemy." He seems to be thinking of home and all the things that he may never see again. On his face are the outlines of many a day of fighting on a bloody battlefield and many a night in a rat-infested foxhole.

The third man is just staring. He has been through so much that his mind can no longer grasp reality. The endless days of seeing his old friends torn down by enemy fire have drained him of all emotion. All he sees now is the desolation that can be the only outcome of war.

On these three men's faces, I see what destruction war can do, not only to men's bodies, but also to their minds. These men will carry the memory of the horror of war with them long after they leave the battlefield.

Contrast the following compositions, one written as straight exposition, the other as "stream of consciousness." Picture on page 116.

The End of the Road

The carnival was closed now. The bright floodlights, the din of the crowds, the gaudy music, and the woody smell of the rides had all disappeared. To take their place was only the clank, thud, and shuffle as the brawny workmen hastily disassembled the mechanisms and the tents; the seats, the food, the sawdust—all were fading away. Several huge trucks had pulled up the ramp and were being loaded with what pieces of equipment the show itself owned. The drivers stayed in the cabs while the hired workmen assailed their duties. On the truck at the left, somewhat apart from the others, two men were engaged in loading a heavy steel horse from the merry-go-round. In the truck one of them, bare-chested, pulled at the top while his friend, sweating in a grease-stained jacket, pushed from the bottom. Their muscles bulged until their charge had been lifted into the truck; they had expended their energy for a moment. To the rear of them, another cart brought more material to be loaded. The men paused for a moment and surveyed the oncoming vehicle. The man at the bottom seemed angry. He was defiantly —yet expectantly—awaiting his future. The man on the truck took a different view. He was calm. He was a big man—and seemed not to care about his next job. He knew he had nothing to fear.

No Strike

Here they come back from the strike negotiations. Those guys are crazy! I've been working on the fair circuit for over five years and I know that they'll never get those benefits that they're asking for. New hydraulic lifts and better housing are just out of the question. Why don't those guys smarten up and realize the facts. Sam and I here, well, we know from experience that that strike stuff just gets you thrown off the lot. They don't realize that the boss is doing them a favor by giving them a job, because otherwise they'd be just ordinary unskilled, unemployed jerks. They don't even know how to put one of those merry-go-round things together. That's why Sam and I are doing it now. I can really laugh at those guys, because they don't even know what they're missing by striking. Yes, I have a good life and I don't complain. I've got money for cigarettes and all the drinks I want, and even some left over. I've got a future and I'm sure glad that I'm not mixed up in no strike!

In attempting to characterize the two roustabouts, both students have been inconsistent in language: at certain points, words suggest one kind of personality, but at other points, a contradictory kind.

The Model

From the very first moment that I saw her, a suspicion grew within me that maybe she really wasn't the detestable person she appeared to be. By everybody she was considered a cruel, thoughtless person, lacking any kindness; but, after I had seen her on very many occasions, I began slowly to discard this popular opinion. There was no doubt that the things she did to people were cruel, but after I became accustomed to her heartless actions, I studied her face and the emotions which others could not seem to perceive. I was surprised and almost delighted as I began to notice day after day an almost imperceptible glitter of compassion, shame, and misery. I saw only these, and to me her other self was only a mechanical impression, a false character.

This short character study, written about the model on page 112, raises the controversial question of meaning: Is that what the picture reveals? Even more important, however, is the other question: Has the writer developed his debatable idea thoroughly and persuasively? Then, compare the following little essay about the two dogs on pages 50–51.

In nature one may find beauty in softness as well as harshness; for example, a common house dog is beautiful; his beauty lies in the softness of his eyes, his large, furry ears, and the touch of sadness at the edge of his mouth. The animal radiates a certain warmth . . . an inexpressible glow . . . as it curls up by the fire. Yet, isn't the sleek, stubbled-haired, muscular type of dog also beautiful? Though his coat of fur does not shine, and his ear are crooked, he still may be deemed a lovely creature; however, it is not because of his attractiveness, but rather his forcefulness and aggressiveness that he is elegant. His pulsating veins, the alert eyes, the hot, panting breath combine to form an image of power and speed . . . an image of beauty.

In the following monologue of the imagined thought
of a soldier seeing the children on page 123, how clearly
is the character of the "thinker" suggested by his word
and what he notices? How accurate is his observation
and how convincing is his imagination? Is the composi
tion "corny"?

Damn This War!

Boy, am I glad that's over! We finally chased the
Germans out of this little Italian village, but no
without a real battle. Most of the village has beer
completely leveled, and what buildings that are stand
ing are just four walls and no roof, and many of the
walls have big holes in them. Like that building over
there. Hey, what's that sound coming out of tha
hole? Sounds like a bunch of kids having a grea
time. I think I'll check this out.

Well, how about that! It is a bunch of kids, play
ing in this rubble-filled alley. Even after all tha
shooting and killing and fear last night, they are
playing this morning. Kids are amazing. Look a
those two boys in the center. The one in the black
skirt-like clothes must have been kidding the one on
crutches, and the one in the white just has to ge
into the act. He's probably just showing off for his
girl friend back in the audience. At least they all
look like they are having fun, even the one on
crutches.

That one little girl leaning against the wall on the right seems to be afraid of me or my gun. Maybe she thinks I'm going to kill her. It just shows you what war will do to a person. In peacetime, or at least before this war, seeing a gun probably wouldn't have bothered her. Now she knows that a gun isn't just a good way of getting food, or, for some people, of having fun, but a good way of killing people. I know just how she feels. The fear she has now when she sees my gun is the same fear I have before a battle begins—a fear of being killed. I can't wait until this war is over, and I suppose she can't either, so just one week will pass without knowing this fear. I suppose some people, like the rest of these kids, have gotten used to this fear, having experienced it so often. But not me, or that little girl. I like her.

I wonder what that bigger girl has in the basket she is holding. I hope it's food for these kids. There isn't much food around these days. The Germans took most of it, and left all these people to starve. We have given them what food we could, but that isn't too much. Maybe after we chase the Germans a little father north, they can do some planting. It's just about the right season. But what will these people do for food until the crops are ready for harvesting? I hope they have some put away someplace where the Germans didn't get at it. We sure can't support them until then. Hey! I wonder where the parents of the kids are at? If they are still alive, then these kids will be all right, but if they were killed . . .

Everything is so confused. Damn this war! If it wasn't for this war, these kids and their parents would be enjoying life with the rest of their families, I could be home with my family, there would be plenty of food for everybody, this fear would never have existed, and all this suffering, death, and wreckage would be happiness, life, with meaning, and a beautiful country with nice homes. Damn this war!

A Fable

(This fable is based on the picture of the cat and the mouse on page 148.)

Once upon a time there lived a cat named Sylvester. One day, as he was making daily patrol of the kitchen, he came upon a mouse named Ernest, who was caught in a trap.

"Help!" pleaded Ernest. "Please set me free."

"Why?" asked Sylvester.

"Don't you like mice?" queried Ernest.

"Sure I like mice," answered Sylvester, licking his

lips and rubbing his fat little belly with his furry paw.

"Well," replied Ernest, undismayed, "I like cats too, and I'd like to be your friend."

"But how do I know you're not a rat?" asked Sylvester.

"Why don't you smell me and find out?" suggested Ernest.

Now the truth was that Sylvester had lost his sense of smell after a spring cold two years before, but he was too ashamed to admit it. So, he sniffed a few times and said, "Well, I guess you're a mouse all right." Then he set him loose and the two became friends.

A few days later, as they were running and playing and singing "Three Blind Dogs," Sylvester complained that he was hungry.

"I know where there is some cheese," said Ernest. "Come on."

Sylvester followed Ernest to the kitchen door, where Ernest told him to stay and keep watch. Ernest went inside to find the cheese.

"Lend me your tail," called Ernest. "I need something to hold on to."

"All right," answered Sylvester, and he stuck out his tail as far as he could.

Suddenly something snapped on Sylvester's tail.

"OW!" he screamed. And on turning around, he found that his tail was caught in a mouse trap.

"My tail is caught! he exclaimed.

"I know," said Ernest, "but I have the cheese." And off he ran as fast as he could to the safety of his hole.

"Why, you weren't a mouse after all," called Sylvester. "You were a rat."

MORAL: A pleading Ernest is a rat in earnest. Or: if you don't know a rat when you smell one, don't stick out your tail.

Champion

He finished his exercises and started to stand up; the Russian gymnast had just completed his series. The loudspeaker blared, "The next contestant is Steven Freeman of America doing . . ." He stood, like a pointer, perfectly motionless, in perfect concentration. Like a large cat stalking its prey he started his approach; he could see the crowd, on either side and to the front, a gigantic wave about to close in. He was close now, and the moment had come for his leap, off he went; he was an eagle pouncing on a rabbit. He hit and he could feel the comforting cold leather meet his hands. His body bent like a fishing pole and whipped around like a fishtailing car; the leather bit into his hands, but it was a solid feeling, something strong. Suddenly it was all done and he vaulted into the air, a falcon. This was the end, a perfect landing and he couldn't miss first place. He relaxed, but was still on guard. He hit and kept his balance, a cat on his four paws. He glanced at the crowd, then at his scores. First place! He slowly strode off, Hail Caesar, King of Rome.

(This is based on the picture of the blurred gymnast on pages 158–159.)

The following composition written on the "face" pictured on page 63 shows how one student saw a comparison and used it to develop his short essay. An entirely different approach is used in the short piece, "Silent Thoughts."

The eyes are the only parts of the face which seem to me to have any human resemblance. The eyelashes and shine of the pupils, and perhaps the shadow over the socket, create the effect of animation. The rest of the face, which has no expression in the sense that the features could change, is unhuman, partly because of the blaring light on the forehead bringing out the baldness, thus taking away something I associate with a face—hair around the head.

This picture reminds me of a picture I saw of a man in France after the last war, whose whole family had been wiped out by the enemy. He had no expression, the only sign of life being in his eyes. Otherwise, his face was an expressionless mask. The disaster had taken from that man all sentiments, and only his eyes remained to show life in his face. So, in a way, does the picture in the book remind me of men I know back home from the woods in Vermont, whose weather-beaten leathery countenances show no feeling, and only their eyes express the workings of their keen minds. In both these comparisons, the lack of sound is impressive. Bleak silence might express the feeling I get from the face in the annual.

Silent Thoughts

He doesn't know what it's like to sit here day after day. Silly, self-important people are always gawking at you; rubbing their fingers over your hair, and nose, and God-knows-what else; and then making those damn snotty cracks as if you were somehow responsible for your appearance. Don't they realize that you just get created? You don't have any say in the matter, do you, mister?

Read the following essay and then see whether you can answer the question at the end.

Freedom is exemption from action, release from pressure, reprieve from punishment. Freedom without determination or responsibility is meaningless. Viewed honestly and without pretense, true freedom is the collapse of all universal laws of responsibility. To be exact, freedom is itself nothingness, and is just as meaningless.

But, freedom with determination is very real. It involves the concept of choice: choice of the particulars of a man's existence—particulars which determine what a man is and what he does with his life. Thus, responsible freedom is not the gift of deity or country. It is an individual's privilege of and liability for, his actions.

According to the most basic doctrines of existentialism, a man's duty is *to* himself, his concern is *for* himself, he is guilty *of* himself, and he *is* his own necessity. Idealistically speaking, it is ignorant to say that a man is determined by his environment, for a man emphasizes, qualifies, restricts, or nullifies his environment by the values he reads into it. Just as slums have produced juvenile delinquents and criminals, equally detestable living conditions have produced great poets, brilliant composers, and financial geniuses.

This is why freedom is dreadful. It is the choice of bringing a purpose out of existence, or making a world out of nothing—through actions (for there is no transcendent "essence of humanity." The actions of men replace this).

The dread lies in the choices a man makes as to the course of his life, and in the awareness that a wrong choice, or no choice at all, can turn his world into nothingness, emptiness, and *self*-annihilation.

Now that you have seen all the pictures in this book, which one do you think stimulated this essay?

This book deliberately focuses on descriptive writing spite the fact that formidable opponents like Ernest emingway advise young writers to throw away their jectives.

All good teachers know what Hemingway means, d this book does not aim at reviving the luscious prose Samuel Taylor Coleridge. It does, however, aim at veloping what might be called a descriptive eye, an e for small, sharp, dramatic detail. Without such vision ere will be very little good writing of any kind, either e Hemingway or Coleridge.

With it, young writers will at least be equipped to stinguish between good and bad description; but what more important, they will have, in the professional's rds, "something to say," and the teacher can fulfill his tural function of showing his students HOW to say it.

Too many textbooks and too many teachers have orked from the incomplete assumption that young iters, particularly in the ninth and tenth grades, should end all their time perfecting their mechanics. As a result, hundreds of high-school graduates can produce comtent expository prose that doesn't say anything worth ading. What is needed is a concentrated effort to show ys and girls how to find interesting subject matter. One ay is to show them how to think; the other, which is the sis of this book, is to teach them how to see.

All good writing is based on a descriptive ability, om the Song of Solomon to Shakespeare to J. D. Salger. It appears even in philosophical and scientific says. Charles S. Peirce, for example, the American scient and philosopher, gave his climactic definition of science in physically descriptive language:

> True science is distinctively the study of useless things. For the useful things will get studied without the aid of scientific men. To employ these rare minds on such work is like running a steam engine by burning diamonds.

221

Mr. Peirce's final phrase illustrates his ability
write abstractly and concretely at the same time, one
the greatest of all literary arts. The fuzziness, the vag
ness of most student writing is due largely to the f
that boys and girls have never learned to observe phy
cally and specifically. They charge heavily into mo
mental abstractions without any conception of how th
intangible ideas relate to our tangible earth. On the c
trary, no one, amateur or professional, can write in
ligently until he has spent years understanding su
relationships.

In a sense, students must pass through a descript
phase before they can be cleared for other, more comp
hensive writing. To emphasize this idea by an analo
description is like physical technique to a musician: it
of limited value by itself, but no important ideas are a
good without it.

The objective of this book is not, therefore, an end
itself; the goal is an expansive one—a way of seei
which will spread through an individual's entire life, fr
thinking to writing, to personal relationships, to studyi
to emotional reactions, and to inspiration. As one prof
sional photographer described it: "In the process of lea
ing my work, I developed an entirely new way of looki
at human experience."

It is not the sloppy, hurried way that most peo
look at pictures, AND life. It is the intense, concentra
way that distinguishes artists, philosophers, and super
men of business: the way of all terse, sensitive, a
thoughtful men and women.

If students will learn to study pictures in the w
advocated in this book, furthermore, no academician
pedagogue will be able to argue, as they so often do, t
"pictures" have destroyed the art of thought, and ha
corrupted language; for nobody who has learned to tra
late accurate, imaginative visual images into precise, su
gestive language can ever be charged as an enemy
verbal expressiveness.

Many teachers discuss visual education as if they
ped pictures were not here to stay. The greater part of
isdom, however, is to accept the inevitable and use it in
e most intelligent, precise, and imaginative way pos-
ble. Throughout this book the controlling conviction is
at the way is to show how vision, thought, and language
e inseparably connected, and that when these connec-
ons are mastered, all three will be forever enriched.

To conclude with a final, practical word: harassed
achers who do not see how they can possibly handle a
t of writing in large classes, can find here a program of
ort, valuable exercises which can be used often without
roducing mountains of papers to correct. A single sen-
nce every day from every student, written from concen-
ated observation, would be an intensely valuable experi-
ice in writing.